I See Circles

D.H. Dilkes

Bailey Books
an imprint of
Enslow Publishers, Inc.
40 Industrial Road
Box 398
Berkeley Heights, NJ 07922
USA

http://www.enslow.com

Bailey Books, an imprint of Enslow Publishers, Inc.

Library of Congress Cataloging-in-Publication Data

Dilkes, D. H.
I see circles / by D.H. Dilkes.
    p. cm. — (All about shapes)
Includes index.
Summary: "Simple text and photographs present a story with a theme about circles"—
Provided by publisher.
ISBN 978-0-7660-3799-1
1. Circle—Juvenile literature. 2. Shapes—Juvenile literature. I. Title.
QA484.D53 2011
516'.152—dc22

                                    2010018400

Paperback ISBN: 978-1-59845-150-4

Printed in the United States of America

052010 Lake Book Manufacturing, Inc., Melrose Park, IL

10 9 8 7 6 5 4 3 2 1

To Our Readers: We have done our best to make sure all Internet Addresses in this book
were active and appropriate when we went to press. However, the author and the publisher
have no control over and assume no liability for the material available on those Internet sites
or on other Web sites they may link to. Any comments or suggestions can be sent by e-mail
to comments@enslow.com or to the address on the back cover.

Photo Credits: Shutterstock.com

Cover Photo: Shutterstock.com

Note to Parents and Teachers

Help pre-readers get a jumpstart on reading. These lively stories introduce simple concepts
with repetition of words and short simple sentences. Photos and illustrations fill the pages
with color and effectively enhance the text. Free Educator Guides are available for this
series at www.enslow.com. Search for the *All About Shapes* series name.

Contents

Words to Know

circle

orange

street

I see circles.

One is in the sky.

One is on
the street.

One is an orange pie.

I see some so small.

A big one for a ball.

One I can bake

and one I can eat.

This one
I can make.

Two to help
me see.

Read More

Olson, Nathan. *Circles Around Town*. Mankato, Minn.: Capstone Press, 2007.

Rau, Dana Meachen. *Circles*. Tarrytown, N.Y.: Marshall Cavendish Benchmark, 2007.

Web Sites

Fisher-Price. *Learn Your Colors and Shapes.*
<http://www.fisher-price.com/us/fun/games/colorshapes/>
Press any key to start!

Kids Learning Station. *Preschool Shapes Worksheets.*
<http://www.kidslearningstation.com/preschool/
shapes-worksheets.asp>
Click on "Circles Worksheet."

Index

Guided Reading Level: **B**
Guided Reading Leveling System is based on the guidelines recommended by Fountas and Pinnell.

Word Count: 45